D1200940

Khan Academy
and Salman Khan

INTERNET BIOGRAPHIES™

Khan Academy
and Salman Khan

ARIANA WOLFF

ROSEN
PUBLISHING®

New York

Published in 2015 by The Rosen Publishing Group, Inc.
29 East 21st Street, New York, NY 10010

Library of Congress Cataloging-in-Publication Data

Wolff, Ariana.
Khan Academy and Salman Khan/Ariana Wolff.—First edition.
  pages cm.—(Internet biographies)
Includes bibliographical references and index.
ISBN 978-1-4777-7927-9 (library bound)
1. Khan, Salman, 1976-–—Juvenile literature. 2. Khan Academy—
Juvenile literature. 3. Internet in education—Juvenile literature.
4. Tutors and tutoring—Computer network resources—Juvenile
literature. 5. Self-culture—Computer network resources—
Juvenile literature. 6. Distance education—Computer network
resources—Juvenile literature. 7. Educational innovations—
History—21st century. 8. Educators—Biography. I. Title.
LB1044.87.W62 2014
371.33'44678—dc23

                                                    2014009018

Manufactured in the United States of America

Contents

INTRODUCTION

Imagine your typical school day. You arrive early in the morning for the first bell after cramming for a quiz on the bus or in your parent's car. You rush to your first-period class, find your seat, and prepare for a long day. It's you and twenty to thirty other students all facing one teacher. Most of the time, you do just fine, but sometimes, a concept confuses you. You want to question your teacher one-on-one, but perhaps the schedule doesn't allow for that, and you and your unanswered question head down the hall to the next class.

For a lot of students, the school day is busy. There simply isn't enough time to put extra focus on anything from specifics to entire subjects that just aren't making sense. Many students find it difficult to add in tutoring

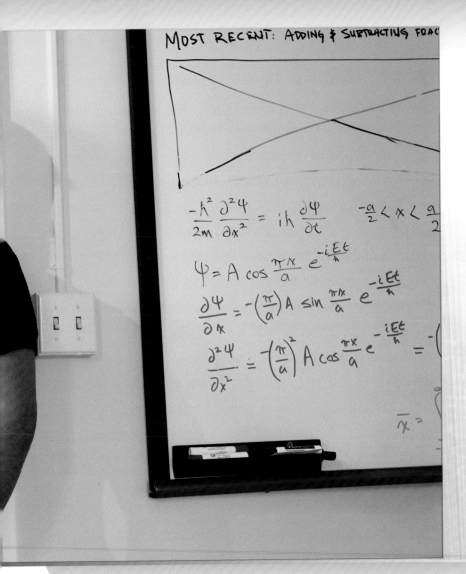

MOST RECENT: ADDING & SUBTRACTING FRAC

$$-\frac{\hbar^2}{2m}\frac{\partial^2 \Psi}{\partial x^2} = i\hbar \frac{\partial \Psi}{\partial t} \qquad -\frac{a}{2} < x < \frac{a}{2}$$

$$\Psi = A \cos \frac{\pi x}{a} \, e^{-\frac{iEt}{\hbar}}$$

$$\frac{\partial \Psi}{\partial x} = -\left(\frac{\pi}{a}\right) A \sin \frac{\pi x}{a} \, e^{-\frac{iEt}{\hbar}}$$

$$\frac{\partial^2 \Psi}{\partial x^2} = -\left(\frac{\pi}{a}\right)^2 A \cos \frac{\pi x}{a} \, e^{-\frac{iEt}{\hbar}} = -$$

$$\overline{x} =$$

Salman Khan is the tutoring techie who transformed his frustrations with the educational system while growing up and throughout college into the Khan Academy, a self-paced, interactive tutoring website.

to an already-packed schedule of classes, extracurricular activities, sports, and a social life. But what if tutoring could happen on *your* terms, on *your* time? Thanks to one visionary techie, learning outside the classroom has been changed forever. That techie is Salman Khan, founder of the Khan Academy.

Khan's childhood wasn't particularly different from how a good number of children in the United States grow up. His parents were immigrants from South Asia who lived near New Orleans, Louisiana. They divorced when Khan was still young, and he grew up with his mother and older sister. He went to public school and did well in his classes, but he found himself increasingly frustrated with certain aspects of the educational system. Even from a young age, Khan asked himself, "Why do some students excel while others fall behind? How can one teacher address the needs of so many students?"

As Khan moved through high school and college, he became increasingly aware that different students learn at different paces and that the traditional classroom setup of one teacher or professor and dozens, if not hundreds, of students was a scenario that left struggling learners out of the equation. It would take Khan's personal experience with a family member in need of academic assistance to realize that he could use the Internet to change education. What started as a small operation tutoring his younger cousin Nadia, who lived 1,500 miles (2,400 kilometers), away turned into an education revolution.

Using the tools of the Internet—instant messaging, screen-sharing software, and YouTube videos—along with his own know-how in computer programming languages, Khan was able to create an interactive tutoring website, the Khan Academy. He started with just a handful of relatives and family friends, but word spread quickly, and soon the Khan Academy had hundreds of views per video. Within a matter of years, Khan left his full-time job in 2009 to focus exclusively on his tutoring gig. A 2011 report by the *New York Times* placed viewership at a whopping 3.5 million users per month. Now Khan is continuing to adapt his teaching model to real-life classrooms, and he is exploring ways to use the Internet to provide education to remote regions where educational opportunities may be scarce. He's also keeping pace with the changing educational landscape. Soon after the College Board stated its intention to redesign the 2016 SATs, the board and the academy announced their partnership and the academy's plan to provide free test-prep materials well in advance of the retooled college entrance exam.

The pages to come will follow Khan's development from a one-man operation using the phone and an online sketch board to help out his twelve-year-old cousin to becoming the director of one of the most innovative nonprofits dedicated to free and accessible learning at a pace customized to each learner's needs. The journey has required hard work, expansive thinking, and ground-breaking creativity, but Salman Khan and the Khan Academy have revolutionized learning—all so that you and millions of others can learn some important lessons, both in school and on your *own* time.

CHAPTER 1

Young Sal Khan, a Self-Paced Learner

Since its initial start-up as a small family tutoring operation, the Khan Academy has grown into an innovative learning model that aims to provide high-quality instruction for any student with a passion for learning, regardless of where that student lives, what his or her background is, or whether or not the would-be student's parents can afford to pay for traditional one-on-one or even group tutoring. Typically, the tech start-ups that create popular Internet websites or apps initially require major financial investments just to get off the ground. What makes the Khan Academy unique—as is abundantly clear throughout its story—is the way it has steadily grown in scale and impact comparable to popular tech companies, all while remaining a relatively small-staffed operation.

Not just any person would have the perfect blend of a tech-savvy mind and the practical understanding of what the average student needs to be able to come up with such

The Khan Academy tutoring model is based on the philosophy of making high-quality instruction available on a student's own time and at his or her own pace.

a simple digital learning method as the Khan Academy provides. When boiled down, it makes sense that the Khan Academy's basic premise of a tutoring model customized for each student and easily accessible for all who wish to access it came from a high-achieving public school student whose parents were hard-working immigrants.

THE AMERICAN DREAM

Salman "Sal" Khan was born on October 11, 1976, in New Orleans, Louisiana. His mother was an immigrant from Calcutta, one of the largest cities in India, and his father was born in the smaller port city of Barisal, in neighboring Bangladesh. Both migrated to the United States, where Sal—the nickname that Khan's friends and family have always called him—was born. His father left the family when Sal was only two years old and moved to Philadelphia, Pennsylvania. Khan's mother worked a range of odd jobs to try and raise both him and his older sister. Sal saw his father only once after he left, when he was twelve years old, before his father passed away when Sal was thirteen years old.

Despite the fact that his father had moved to Philadelphia and could not afford to send child support, Sal has fond memories of his upbringing. His mother worked very hard, and according to an interview with Khan published by the United Kingdom–based newspaper the *Telegraph* on September 28, 2012, "there was always food on the table." His childhood circumstances weren't easy, but growing up as he did taught Khan an extremely valuable lesson. As he recalls, "We lived at the poverty line and I was on free school lunches. My mother is always very embarrassed when I say that, but I love that about this country [the United States]: people don't care where you come from." From an early age, Khan understood that one's background didn't matter. He sensed that anyone could achieve a better life by combining hard work and determination.

As a child, Khan attended Phoebe Hearst Elementary School in Metairie, Louisiana, where he excelled academically. In a 2013 interview for the New Orleans–based *Times-Picayune*, he recalls being separated from the rest of his class and put into a group of accelerated students where he could proceed to learn at his own pace. According to Khan, the sense of freedom that he felt was notable, even at nine years of age. In his own words, the independent study model "allowed for [his] natural curiosity not to be squashed." He began to think that the traditional classroom setup of a teacher in front of a blackboard facing a group of silent students "suppresses something."

All of Khan's early experiences in public school observing the differences that existed in such a diverse group of students—some who excelled academically and others who were often left discouraged—left him with ample ideas about the problems with public education and the various ways in which it could be improved. In the very same halls walked children who excelled academically alongside others who were disinterested and largely overlooked by their teachers. Even at such a young age, Khan knew there was a major flaw in how students were being taught. Nonetheless, he did not have a clear career path yet, nor did he realize that these experiences would some day cause him to revolutionize learning.

"TESTING OUT"

As a teenager, Salman Khan attended Grace King High School, where his experiences with the public education system continued to leave their mark. By this point, he was performing exceptionally well as a math student— so well, in fact, that he joined his school's competitive math team, commonly called the "mathletes." These teams travel to competitions where students seek to prove their proficiency by solving mathematics equations quicker and more accurately than students at other schools.

In his book on education reform and his own story, *The One World Schoolhouse: Education Reimagined*, Khan describes a defining encounter for him at one of the regional mathematics competitions that he attended with his team in Louisiana. There, he met Shantanu Sinha, an accelerated student from another high school who defeated him in the finals round of the competition. After the defeat, the two students exchanged experiences and Shantanu planted an important seed in Salman's head.

Both students were in tenth grade, yet while Salman was stuck in an Algebra II course that, according to him, "had ceased to be stimulating," Shantanu's school had allowed him to move forward to pre-calculus. Salman was astonished and asked how he had done it. Shantanu simply told him that he tested out of Algebra II, so his school let him move forward to pre-calculus.

The concept of "testing out" of a class seemed novel to Salman—and logical, too. In his own elementary

Many of Sal Khan's observations of classmates at Grace King High School in Metairie, Louisiana, fueled his passion for education reform. Here, he gives the keynote address at the 2013 graduation ceremony.

school experience, he had experienced the benefits of progressing from a classroom where he was often bored and performing better than his peers to a program for gifted students where he was allowed more freedom

to explore school topics at his own pace. If he was surpassing the other students in his algebra class, why shouldn't he just "test out" to pre-calculus? In his words, "if a student could demonstrate proficiency with a certain set of ideas or processes, why not let him or her move on to more advanced ones?"

When Salman returned to his own school after the mathematics competition, he approached the administration with his pitch to advance forward to the next math class. To his great dismay, they turned him down, explaining that if they allowed him to advance out of algebra, they would have to give any student who wished to do so the same opportunity. He was unsatisfied with the answer but resigned himself to sticking it out in Algebra II.

MATHletes Challenges

Mathematics competitions are contests held for students from elementary school through high school and even college. Talented math scholars are tested on their ability to solve a series of equations in a limited amount of time. Different competitions vary in their rules and structure, but they all generally look for the brightest students in the field of math who can solve problems quickly and correctly.

Some of the first recorded competitions date back to Europe at the end of the ninteenth century. But today, they have become much more standardized contests to determine the best math students worldwide. In the last hundred years, these competitions have become a widely popular extracurricular activity for students who love math, and there is even a special name for someone who competes in these competitions: a mathlete. When he was in high school, Salman Khan was quite the mathlete!

The largest organized mathematics competition in the United States is the American Mathematics Competitions (AMC). Winners of the AMC travel to represent the United States in the International Mathematical Olympiad (IMC). In other countries, such as Canada, the United Kingdom, and Japan, there are similar processes to select talented students. In 2014, the Irish technology entrepreneur Sean O'Sullivan announced a new competition called the MATHletes Challenge. This new challenge is based on the principles of the Khan Academy, and students across Ireland are able to participate online via the Khan Academy website.

Khan's story of meeting Shantanu Sinha shows the positive impact that extracurricular learning can have on a student and how interaction with others in learning serves a great purpose. The value of his personal experiences would become very notable in Khan's later work in education.

Irish entrepreneur and investor Sean O'Sullivan has been a major financial backer of the Khan Academy. In 2014, he announced the MATHletes Challenge hosted on the Khan Academy website.

Later in high school, Salman found a way to work around the math rules at his school: he took summer courses at a local college until his own school allowed him to advance to basic calculus. The experience solidified his stance that self-paced learning was a key element to student success and the traditional public school teaching methodology undervalued the importance of independent study. He attributes much of his drive and success to his mother's support and that his community placed a high degree of importance on education. Still, he couldn't help but wonder what happened to those students who weren't so fortunate.

STUDENTS TO TEACHERS: A TOP-HEAVY FRACTION

Given his academic drive and self-motivated studies, it isn't surprising that Salman graduated valedictorian at Grace King High School, nor that he achieved a perfect score on the math portion of his SAT. These successes led him to the Massachusetts Institute of Technology (MIT), where he would meet his former mathlete competitor Shantanu Sinha once again, becoming close friends and roommates.

While high school life was dictated by a strict schedule and teacher-run routine, college proved more liberating, with more independence for students and flexibility in their course selection and use of time. Salman felt the effects. He and Shantanu would often observe that while the lure of famed Nobel Prize–winning professors or the sheer guilt of skipping massive lectures drew many of their peers into class attendance, the massive "broadcast lectures" were boring. They also noticed that the types of students who persistently attended these lectures were the very ones cramming for exams and feeling overwhelmed by the material.

Salman slowly reached the conclusion that sitting passively in a classroom didn't advance anybody's education. He realized that the best use of his time was in independent learning, relying on his professors and peers for consultation, debate, or discussion. The lessons he had learned from elementary and high school trickled through to college, where his proactive use of time and resources led him to graduate with a high grade point average (GPA) and three degrees: a bachelor's in mathematics and both a bachelor's and a master's in computer science and electrical engineering. He would go on to obtain a master of business administration (MBA) degree from Harvard University as well.

All of his educational experiences through college led him to understand something important about the education system in place: despite what could have been a disadvantageous background in coming from a working-class family, coupled with certain educators who restricted his ability to study as he pleased, he always achieved more success than did his peers when he put in the effort and found the means to work around the traditional classroom model of one teacher lecturing to many students. He never considered himself necessarily smarter or a harder worker; he simply found innovative ways to work around what he saw as an imperfect system.

The experiences that Khan had growing up would profoundly influence his take on education, but fresh out of a business program at Harvard and without a clear direction in the world of education, Khan followed his natural course and became a hedge fund analyst, somebody who analyzes data on finances and budgets for clients and makes recommendations on how to manage their funds. It would only be a few years later while tutoring a younger cousin online that Khan's passion for alternative education models would reemerge and take him in a new direction.

CHAPTER 2

Tutoring Across Time Zones

It was in 2004 that a twenty-eight-year-old Salman Khan, employed at the time as a successful hedge fund analyst, would begin tutoring his younger cousin, Nadia, in math. Having been successful in his personal studies of mathematics throughout elementary, middle, and high school, as well as in college, Khan was a no-brainer choice as a tutor for his seventh-grade cousin. There was, however, one obvious dilemma that presented itself to their tutoring arrangement: Khan was still living in Boston after college, while Nadia was living back in his home state of Louisiana. Khan came up with the idea to use Yahoo! Messenger's Doodle service as a way to cross the logistical divide.

DOODLING THE WAY TO AN "A"

Yahoo! Messenger (commonly called just "Messenger") is an instant messaging client created by the Internet web

Yahoo! Messenger (https://messenger.yahoo.com) launched in 1998 as a popular chat client and IM service. Salman Khan used its platform to tutor his younger cousin at a distance.

directory and search engine Yahoo! It was initially launched as an online chat client in 1998, allowing users in different locations to communicate with each other via short messages sent back and forth online in real time. One of the more popular features the instant messenger provides is IMVironments (a clever play on the abbreviation "IM"—instant message—and the word "environments"). According to the Yahoo! website, IMVironments, or "IMVs" for short, are "interactive backgrounds that you can add to your IM conversations."

Instant Messaging

With the developments that have occurred in communications since the Internet first became widely available for home use, it can be hard to imagine the impact instant messaging (IM) has had on Internet communication. Nonetheless, before chat clients developed online real-time text, the average Internet user who was far away from someone for whom he or she had a message needed to wait for an e-mail to be delivered and opened. The fact that Wi-Fi and other forms of wireless Internet such as 4G weren't widely available until the first decade of the 2000s, coupled with the common delays in Internet connection speeds (many users used dial-up Internet access, which operated over public phone lines at speeds much slower than technology today permits), often meant a simple conversation could be dragged out over an entire day or even multiple days.

Instant messaging was a major step toward allowing Internet users in remote locations to communicate back and forth instantaneously. With instant messaging, the text that one user keyed in could appear on the other user's screen immediately, making it simple to have a two-way

(continued on the next page)

(continued from the previous page)

conversation. While many users would simply chat with their friends or catch up with family who lived far away, real-time chat became an important tool that would eventually give way to other opportunities, such as digital tutoring in the case of Salman Khan and his cousin Nadia.

Doodle is an IMV that allows users to draw images on screen, visible to the other party in the chat.

When Khan agreed to tutor his younger cousin Nadia from a distance, he had the innovative idea of using Yahoo! Doodle to share a notepad with his new student. He would call Nadia on the phone to explain the exercises while employing the digital canvas to write out otherwise-difficult-to-type math equations, as well as drawing out visual examples to help demonstrate tougher, more conceptual ideas. His tutoring method was highly successful. Nadia thrived in math, and Khan was soon convinced to help tutor Nadia's brothers, Ali and Arman.

As could be expected, Nadia's brothers also thrived, and other relatives soon jumped on board, asking Khan to assist in their studies as well. In order to keep up with the demands of his now-numerous students, Khan wrote a JavaScript language that would generate practice problems. JavaScript is a computer programming language that he was able to use to program an automatic problem generator on his own website. The use of an automatic problem generator helped alleviate the need for Khan to personally develop multiple practice problems for students at varying levels of math.

Another key step that Khan took to help handle the new increase in students was organizing all of the content on his website. As he accumulated more relatives and family friends as students, he grouped the content and problems on

```
<script language="javascript">
     Event.observe(window, 'load', init, false)
     function init() {
          Lightbox.init();

     }

</script>

<script language="javascript">
function sprawdz_add_product(this){
     turn(false);
          ..wdz add_customer(this){
```

JavaScript is a computer programming language commonly used in web browsers to create interactive user interfaces. Khan used JavaScript to create an automatic problem generator for his early students.

his website into modules, or independent units of study on a specific topic, also creating a database to track the progress of each of his students. This seemingly simple move was actually part of the ingenious methodology that Khan has consistently put into practice. His success has always been a result of combining the Internet and the tools it offers with education to form a successful model for tutoring.

BLUEPRINT FOR SOMETHING BIGGER

Despite the initial success that Khan was having with Yahoo! Doodle, scheduling so many different students soon became an issue for him. As he tutored multiple relatives, he still kept his full-time job as a senior analyst at Wohl Capital Management, the hedge fund where he had started working after graduating from Harvard. The time constraints of attempting to work his regular job and tutor so many different relatives at different levels of math—not to mention the difference in time zones between where Khan and each of his students lived—was proving too difficult to maintain.

A friend of Khan's suggested that he try recording videos. The friend thought it would be a good idea to upload them to the video-hosting service YouTube, where they would remain available for anybody to watch when they needed. On YouTube, any user can log on and watch videos that other users have posted to the site at their own convenience. This move would allow Khan to record his

The hand-drawn math problems that Khan created on Yahoo! Doodle proved so approachable and effective that they've continued to form a key part of the Khan Academy's lessons to this day.

lessons whenever he found the time in his schedule, and his cousins and their friends would subsequently be able to watch them in their own free time.

In a 2014 interview with the *New York Times*, Khan explained that his initial reaction was quite dismissive. He recalls saying, "That's a horrible idea. YouTube is for cats playing piano." In his mind, YouTube was a place for entertainment and comedy videos; it didn't seem like the proper format for scholarly learning. Nonetheless, true to style, Khan tried to see the bigger picture. After all, he was the math tutor using Yahoo! Doodle to illustrate practice problems and calculations.

Khan gave in and decided to try the creative solution: he started recording his Doodle lessons as videos in which a viewer could watch a screenshot of his digital "blackboard" while listening to his recorded voiceovers explaining the math problems in progress. (A screenshot is an image of the screen display on a computer, television, phone, or other visual output device.) Khan himself didn't visibly appear in the videos, just his drawings and notes.

The move to keep himself out of the videos was smart, considering it could have turned out to be boring and too similar to the traditional classroom model he begrudged so much as a student. Instead, Khan used a program to record a screenshot of his own computer's monitor as he drew out the problems, effectively turning the screen into a workspace itself. Coupled with Khan's explanations, which were delivered in a friendly tone, the results were simple yet thorough clips in which each lesson was presented both visually and aurally. With this technique, Khan found the potential to replicate the one-on-one tutoring experience online without requiring both parties to be simultaneously present.

YOUTUBE BECOMES YOURTUTOR

A lot of the simplicities of Khan's early videos were really just fortuitous consequences of his circumstances in that initial stage. On the one hand, there was the simple limitation of funding. Unlike a major tutoring institute, Khan was one person making videos in his free time at home. His original studio was actually only a closet, equipped with a desktop computer just like anyone could buy at an electronics store, a Wacom graphic tablet (a compact computer input device) on which he could draw math exercises with an electronic pen, screenshot software to record what appeared on the monitor, and a microphone that he ordered online. This fairly simple setup understandably led to videos that seemed relatively amateurish. They were indeed low-tech doodles, but with an encouraging voice that made math easy to understand.

Another early restraint that proved to be to Khan's benefit was the length of the videos. Khan posted his first one on November 16, 2006, at a time when YouTube still limited the length of videos it would host to ten minutes or less. As a result, Khan kept the videos brief. Each video tried to address a specific topic in that time limit (the first posted on the basics of least common multiples), after which the viewer could do practice exercises on the website to test his or her learning. Eventually, YouTube began to host videos longer than the ten-minute cap it had enforced earlier, but Khan kept his videos to a ten-to-fifteen-minute maximum. Compared to an hour-long lecture at school, the short clips had better potential to keep a student's attention.

Khan attributes much of his early success to the YouTube video-hosting service. In 2006, the cost of hosting streaming videos online was much higher than it would later become, and Khan asserts that he couldn't have afforded a server large enough for the number of videos he was uploading. Private video hosting would also have limited the amount of traffic he could receive. Even though Khan was uploading the videos expecting only relatives and family friends to log on and watch, the videos quickly became popular, gaining a following from among various YouTube users. Many wrote him notes insisting he had helped them pass exams or otherwise succeed in their math classes.

Quickly, a handful of students had become thousands, and the number continued to increase. Khan continued working as a financial analyst, but after a few years he found the Khan Academy growing to numbers beyond any initial expectations. A difficult economic downturn in 2008, coupled with the time constraints of balancing his day job as a financial analyst with the ever-expanding academy, led Khan to leave his full-time job at the hedge fund that year. He briefly attempted to start up his own fund, but the economic climate wasn't ripe for hedge funds, and his own business didn't take off. That was when he decided to dedicate himself full-time to his educational videos. He and his wife, Umaima, used savings to buy a house, and the surplus became the start-up funding for Khan's new full-time job at the Khan Academy.

His new working arrangement was, at times, difficult (Khan was living off of savings and not charging users to view his videos). However, Khan's ability to create a tutoring alternative by channeling his own experiences as a student into the Khan Academy's teaching style—as well as the positive feedback from commenters on his YouTube videos—made the academy the clear path for him.

In fact, this ability Khan demonstrated so early in his educational work to adapt those aspects of traditional learning models that he felt worked—problem solving, measures of progress, and the human factor, as opposed to learning from a book, to name a few—with the optimal software and tools the Internet offered has consistently proven to be

EAKTHROUGH

The support of Salman Khan's wife, Umaima—both emotional and financial—proved important when Khan decided to ditch the finance world and focus on the Khan Academy full-time.

the key factor in the success of the Khan Academy. This ingenious blend along with Khan's skill at determining proactive means to overcome obstacles, such as the physical distance separating him from his cousin Nadia, or the use of YouTube to avoid high costs or a crashing server, are how the Khan Academy made the leap from a small family operation to the most popular YouTube channel for educational videos.

CHAPTER 3

The Khan Approach

While on paper the Khan Academy can be described as a nonprofit educational organization seeking to provide a free education to anyone who wants to learn, this description obviously doesn't give the full picture of what the real user experience is like. The heart of the academy is its website (although it has grown to develop other offline projects as well, which will be addressed later). The website—at www.khanacademy.org—hosts Salman Khan's video clips, practice exercises, and a variety of tools that users can apply to track their individual progress.

Both highly interactive and carefully structured, the Khan Academy's online curriculum aims to make any given subject area approachable and understandable for each person. In contrast to traditional classroom learning, members on the website can learn at their own pace, have a certain (although not unlimited) degree of freedom to choose which topics they would like to study at a given time, and receive great encouragement not just for succeeding but also for pursuing new areas of knowledge and more difficult tasks. More challenging problems are not made immediately available to every user, but with diligence and patience, a student can move forward, unlocking new topics and progressing through the site's vast material.

GETTING STARTED

A brand new user who logs on to www.khanacademy.org will first be asked to sign up for the website. This first step

New York City–based high school student Jack Parker joined the Khan Academy website to improve his math skills. First-time users must create a profile, which the site uses to track progress and performance in learning modules.

of creating a profile is important, given that the entire emphasis of the Khan Academy's style of learning is that it is customized to each student's needs. By creating a profile, the website is able to track a user's progress, including which tests he or she takes, performance and results, and even how long an individual spends on a given lesson or module. New visitors can sign up with an e-mail address or by linking the site to their existing Facebook or Google account. Teenagers or younger students, especially those under the age of thirteen, can create accounts with the help of their parents.

After creating an account, the site presents a welcome video in which, unlike the actual tutoring videos that have made the site famous, Khan appears on camera and shares basic details about how the Khan Academy works, doing so in a friendly, laid-back tone. His easygoing manner is one of the hallmark features of the academy. The speaker isn't difficult to understand, and most people—both young and old—can connect to him.

Following Khan's introductory video, there is a pretest, which assesses a number of math skills. The pretest presents a series of math problems for which answers should be keyed in and submitted. If a student hasn't learned the material necessary to answer a question, he or she can simply click on a button that reads, "I haven't learned this yet." Just like the concept of "testing out" that Khan had heard about from his fellow mathlete and

Right from the site's introductory video, Khan Academy users become familiar with Khan's face and laid-back tone—integral parts of the website's approach to engaging students.

competitor, Shantanu Sinha, this pretest allows more advanced students to test out of the more elementary topics that they may have already covered in a classroom with their teachers. Thus, even from the first set of problems, the Khan Academy customizes the content that each person faces, designing it especially for an individual's background and skills.

After completing the basic math pretest, the site calculates a student's strengths and weaknesses on the basis of over five hundred unique math skills. A progress bar on the right side of the page will always let a user know which skills he or she has mastered. It will also explain how well he or she has progressed with each particular skill by filling in that skill's corresponding box with a lighter or darker shade of blue. Light blue indicates a lower level of experience, while darker blue indicates having frequently practiced or even mastered a skill.

The goal is for each person with a profile on the website to become aware of where his or her strengths and weaknesses are as the site customizes the content and order of modules to help empower each learner. Some of the skills are more elementary, such as "1-digit addition" or "multiplication with carrying," while others are more advanced, such as "factoring quadratics" or "trigonometry." The site has content covering everything from elementary school math to topics often not seen until late high school or college, including calculus and differential equations.

PRESENTATION IS EVERYTHING

As noted in Khan's introductory video, one of the most acclaimed features of the Khan Academy website is the consistently encouraging tone it uses. This positive and boosting approach isn't reserved for his narration in the videos. The text of the site itself encourages users greatly as well.

Instead of doing lessons as "courses" or receiving grades, such as the letter or 4.0-based grades usually seen on high school report cards, those who sign up for the Khan Academy are invited to embark on "missions," receiving different badges for the successful completion of skill sets. Sometimes they can receive a badge just for trying to tackle a new skill, even if they don't pass the exercises.

One New York City high school senior named Jack Parker says, "I find myself more enthused to study with the Khan Academy than I do with traditional homework… The pace of Sal's presentation is definitely different than my teacher's pace. Not only is Sal's delivery slower and more comprehensible, you can also rewind it if you miss anything." This enthusiastic attitude has been a huge factor in the academy's success.

Another key aspect of the website's approach and success is its emphasis on the pure pursuit of knowledge. Even students who are not performing as well as would be necessary to pass a traditional class in school are rewarded for continuing to try and expand their knowledge. "Energy points" can be earned on the website simply for exploring new subject areas. The idea is that each individual can move at his or her own pace as long as he or she consistently tries and is willing to explore new topics.

When it was founded, the main content on the Khan Academy website focused on STEM materials—that is, topics in the fields of science, technology, engineering, and mathematics (the initials of the word "STEM" are an acronym for these four subject areas). Since then, however, content has expanded into the humanities—including lessons on history, civics, and art history—as well as economics and finance.

While some students have reacted well to the new topics, others are not as trusting of teachers other than Khan himself. Interviewee Jack Parker states, "I have grown to trust and respect [Khan], and I look to *him* to be the teacher." Understandably, it is difficult to teach art history in the same way as math, but the Khan Academy is still seeking the best ways to teach new subject areas in a similar, video-based format.

Another major development has been that much of the content has come to be shaped around standardized testing in the hopes of providing free preparation for important exams that weigh heavily on a student's future. One of the most exciting developments for the Khan Academy since its

Earn Your Badges

The Khan Academy uses a system of badges and energy points to reward users for their progress. There are six different badges:

1. Meteorite badges
2. Moon badges
3. Earth badges
4. Sun badges
5. Black Hole badges
6. Challenge Patches

Each type of badge is reserved as a reward for a different type of challenge. For example, Meteorite badges are the easiest to earn and can be achieved quickly after joining the site. Some of the meteorite badges include "Making Progress," awarded for mastering seven unique skills, or "Fingers or Toes," earned after completing ten practice tasks.

The Moon, Earth, Sun, and Black Hole badges are more difficult to achieve, each corresponding with tasks that require more dedication or modules completed. They are given to users who have completed a high number of tasks, have consistently worked on

(continued on the next page)

Jack Parker browses the different types of Khan Academy badges. The Khan Academy's badge system rewards students both for accuracy as well as for effort and participation in discussions, a reward many find more encouraging than traditional test grades.

(continued from the previous page)

a skill set, or have watched extensive video on a particular topic.

Unlike traditional grades in a classroom setting, Khan Academy badges aren't reserved for students who have performed exceedingly well. While there are badges that reward accuracy, many are given out simply for trying challenging practice problems or engaging in discussion boards.

Challenge patches are given out for achieving mastery in all skills in a particular subject area. The badge system is an integral part of the Khan Academy's effort to make learning fun and encourage students to learn at their own pace.

Jack Parker, the high school senior interviewed for this book, states, "I really like this method because it highlights my victories instead of my failures." Data from the Khan Academy does, in fact, seem to show that students respond well to badges and move on to more problem sets or videos after earning a new badge.

beginning has been new partner content provided by some of the biggest institutions in a variety of fields, including the Museum of Modern Art and the Stanford University School of Medicine, among others.

SKILLS AND MODULES

In any given subject area, a user works through what are known as modules. For example, an early module in the fifth-grade math lessons covers fractions. The module is divided into particular skills: adding and subtracting fractions, word problems on adding and subtracting fractions, multiplying fractions, dividing fractions, and word problems on multiplying fractions. For any given skill, there are a series of videos that seek to explain the content, followed by practice problems designed to help a student achieve mastery of that skill.

Just as it was in the early days of the Khan Academy, when all the videos were designed only for Salman Khan's cousins and family friends, students are still first presented with short ten- to fifteen-minute videos in which Khan explains a basic principle using his digital blackboard. One of the classic marks of the Khan Academy has been that, even as it grows in size and impact to numbers initially unimaginable, the format has remained fairly

Exceeding the limitations of any textbook, Khan Academy modules combine video, text, and quizzes for a multi-format approach. Here, Jack Parker watches one of Khan's videos in which angles are drawn with an electronic pen, just as Khan used to do for his cousin Nadia on Yahoo! Doodle.

consistent. Khan's videos still use an electronic pen that gives his videos a homemade, handwritten look. His tone remains informal and unrehearsed in a way that makes the lessons relatable to students of any age.

Khan's on-screen "handwriting" with the electronic pen illustrates concepts in as clear and simple a way as possible. While somebody who has already mastered a particular skill might find its corresponding video boring, a huge factor in the Khan Academy's success is how it presents any given topic as if the viewer had no prior knowledge. Whether it is a new learner or somebody who may have forgotten a fundamental concept, the videos are designed to teach from scratch and encourage the viewer. This has been a major source of the program's reach.

CRITICISMS OF THE DIGITAL APPROACH

While the Khan Academy's approach to learning has been a major inspiration, and media coverage often highlights what has been described as a revolutionary force in the field of education, many features to which the academy owes its success have been criticized.

One of the most significant markers that most journalists and fans point to when they speak of the Khan Academy's success is the sheer number of users logging on each day to view videos. A 2010 article on CNNMoney.com cited around two hundred thousand people logging onto the website in any given month, although that number has grown even higher in the intervening years, and there are still students who view Khan's lessons on YouTube, as opposed to the academy site. Nonetheless, there have always been major criticisms of the Khan Academy's approach.

One of the most fundamental disapprovals many cite of the Khan Academy's methodology is that Salman Khan lacks training as a classroom teacher. While many hail his "big brother" approach—the fact that he seems more like a friendly tutor than a traditional teacher—others feel that the Khan Academy would benefit from the research of experts in the fields of teaching and adolescent development. Those who study this area of knowledge (called pedagogy) are interested in the ways that students best learn and how a teaching curriculum can be shaped to fit those learning patterns.

Khan has directly stated that he is not interested in studying pedagogy. He has stated that he prefers to directly post videos and observe the feedback to them and user performance on their corresponding exercises as a means of determining which types of videos work well. Nevertheless, this approach has been controversial for those educators who believe strongly in research on learning and the benefits it can provide to an educational curriculum.

Another issue that some critics have pointed out in the Khan Academy approach has been errors or inconsistencies in the videos. Despite the site's growth since its earliest days, most of its content still consists of Khan on his own with the camera and microphone, drawing out practice problems. This lack of oversight means that whenever Khan makes a mistake, that mistake makes it onto the website.

In June 2012, a popular video created by two teachers pointed out each mistake that occurred in one of the videos on multiplying and dividing negative numbers. They claimed that these types of errors were common in all of the Khan Academy videos and ranged from simple inconsistencies in notation to a lack of explanation of why certain mathematical operations occur as they do. In response, the academy pulled the video offline and shot an updated version of the same, implementing the corrections.

Beyond errors in notation, what these two teachers largely criticized in the Khan Academy approach was that it is too procedural—too focused on the steps to solving a problem—and not conceptual enough. In other words, they felt the videos focus on the small steps and rules of mathematics in order to teach students to solve exercise problems and perform well on tests, but that they do not focus on the broader concepts the math problems represent or when to apply them in the real world.

Khan has argued the opposite. In response to the criticisms in the aforementioned video, he claimed the site does indeed host conceptual videos that explain the basis of the procedures. Nonetheless, he still argues that as a student, he learned mathematics from procedural, worked problems and insists that it is the correct focus for a math learning model. In the Khan Academy approach, working through practice problems first is the key to developing a broader understanding of the concepts behind math.

While the Khan Academy method has proven controversial for some, it quickly garnered a high degree of media attention, drawing in many followers. Despite occasional inaccuracies, the quickly growing user base indicated that there was something successful in the academy's method, as students continued to flock to the site to supplement their classroom learning. Khan never imagined his videos would receive any of this attention, but the biggest shock was soon to come when another tech genius would back the project.

CHAPTER 4

The Gates Seal of Approval

B y 2009, the software that Salman Khan had written to generate practice problems for his younger cousins, as well as the YouTube videos that he was recording on rudimentary equipment in a closet of his house, had already well exceeded any of his expectations. In his 2012 book, *The One World Schoolhouse: Education Reimagined*, Khan says, "I didn't dream of creating a popular website or of being a flash-in-the-pan entry in the education debate ... I dreamed of creating something enduring and transformative, an institution for the world."

TOUGH TIMES FOR A TECHIE

By the time Khan made the decision to leave his hedge fund job and direct his full attention to the Khan Academy, tens of thousands of students were watching his lessons daily. That's the good news. The bad news is that

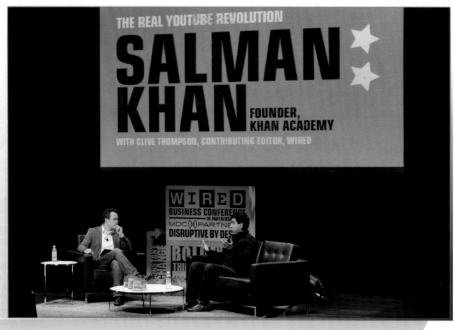

As time progressed, Khan's videos began to draw increasingly greater attention, and as YouTube views skyrocketed, the Khan Academy became a familiar name in the tech industry, particularly among those tuned in to the growth of the YouTube platform.

his $50 a month web host was frequently crashing due to the high traffic. While the Khan Academy's name implied a grandiose operation, in reality, it was still just Salman Khan in his closet with a few hundred dollars' worth of equipment.

He recalls times being quite difficult for his family in that first year he worked exclusively on the Khan Academy. In his book, he says that he "spent most of [his] days in a $6 T-shirt and sweatpants, talking to a computer monitor." After all, the budget for the Khan Academy at that point was in reality just Khan's savings from his prior job. Khan was using up about $5,000 a month from his savings, and the financial strain was adding stress to his marriage and life as a new father. Nonetheless, like many before him who envisioned making a difference, Khan stayed determined to grow his academy. The first sign of relief came in early 2010.

By January 2010, the Khan Academy had become popular enough that other names in the tech industry had heard of the program. Many engineers and executives at Google, the high-traffic search engine, had begun to use the Khan Academy to tutor their own kids. That month, they invited Salman Khan to meet with them. About ten people from the Google staff came to the meeting.

Khan presented screenshots and testimonials about the academy and explained to the Google representatives how his site operated. He also explained the vision that he was fine-tuning: the idea of a free virtual school, customized to each individual's needs based on the data of his or her performance. The small audience seemed sympathetic, but there wasn't any great indication of which direction this meeting would end up taking the Khan Academy, if any. Nevertheless, Google invited Khan back for a second get-together.

At that follow-up meeting, Google posed an interesting question for the one-man show behind the small-time operation that the Khan Academy had been up until that point: what would he do with a $2 million investment? They asked Khan to write a proposal, which he did.

In his proposal, Khan delineated the software engineers whom he would hire, the increase in content he could provide, and the projected impact that this investment would have in terms of users and numbers. After a few months, however, and nothing more than continued talk that Google was looking into his proposal (but had yet to send any funding), Khan came to doubt that he would ever see a real result from those meetings. Still, he remained determined and pushed forward to create new videos for his website.

AN UNEXPECTED ALLY

An important part of Salman Khan's story is that whenever he was discouraged from thinking outside of the box or was faced with difficulties in his attempts to do so, he resisted the temptation to throw in the towel. Rather, he pushed forward. This kind of determination is how he was able to convince his high school to let him take college courses, even though it didn't offer such a program at the time. It was also his approach when he wanted to tutor young Nadia, a thousand miles away. Like many Internet visionaries, Khan looked beyond the expected ways of doing things and was determined to find alternatives. This was the same approach he took with his business.

The initial lack of funding and continued stress that the Khan Academy was putting on his personal life would not dampen Khan's spirit. While nothing financial had emerged from his meetings with Google, they did serve to help him refine his vision. He began to think practically about what the Khan Academy could become with enough funding and a game plan. With the right support, Khan now knew how he could grow his idea and continue to make use of the Internet to reach more students.

Before anything was to emerge from his proposal to Google, Khan received an e-mail from another, unexpected donor. He didn't recognize the name, but in early 2010, a woman named Ann Doerr had written to Khan claiming to be a huge fan and inquiring about where she could send a donation check. Khan was used to receiving small donations online, so he wasn't too surprised that a fan would want to help out. When a $10,000 check arrived in the mail, however, he was quite pleasantly surprised.

A quick online search led Khan to realize that his newest donor was in fact the wife of the famous venture capitalist John Doerr. Since the 1980s, John Doerr has been a key figure in channeling funds to many of the most famous websites and companies in the world, including the popular online retailer Amazon and even Google. Given her husband's history of a keen eye for innovative new ideas, it's not surprising that Ann saw potential in the

Khan Academy and wanted to make a substantial monetary contribution.

After receiving the donation, Khan wrote to Doerr to thank her profusely for her generosity. She suggested

John Doerr is a well-known venture capitalist who has backed some of the biggest names in tech—including Netscape, Amazon, and Google—since the early days of the web. His wife, Ann Doerr, was one of Khan's biggest early supporters.

that the two meet for lunch to discuss the academy and its operations. Few found it easy to believe that the Khan Academy really was such a modest operation. When Doerr asked how Khan was supporting himself and his family,

he uncomfortably explained that they were living off of his savings. Doerr didn't show much of a reaction, but by the time Khan made it home, she had sent him a text message insisting he needed to support himself. A $100,000 donation check was soon on the way to Khan from the Doerrs!

BIG IDEAS AND A BIG SHOUT-OUT

Ann Doerr's support of the Khan Academy, both financial and otherwise, proved to be deeply helpful. Once Google had expressed interest and Doerr had made a hefty donation, Salman Khan started to believe more in the practicality of his goals with the Khan Academy. The Doerr donations were, in effect, tantamount to a Khan Academy badge. What's more, it seems that Doerr's support would kick off a chain of events that took the academy from a project already exceeding Khan's wildest expectations to the center of a media blitz focused on an education revolution.

The Aspen Ideas Festival is an annual weeklong event held in Aspen, Colorado, with discussions, seminars, and panels on a variety of topics, including politics, economics, the arts, and education. In the spring of 2010, a colleague of Bill Gates e-mailed him about the Khan Academy. Gates is the cofounder of the personal computer company Microsoft, a philanthropist, and one of the wealthiest people in the world. He became a fan of the Khan Academy videos and began using them with his then eleven-year-old son, Rory. Later that year, at the 2010 Aspen Ideas Festival, Gates mentioned Salman Khan and the Khan Academy in his responses at a question-and-answer session.

The question posed by the interviewer, writer and biographer Walter Isaacson, was quite open. Isaacson asked, "What can we do to improve K–12 education in America the best?" Gates's initial response reflected that as technology advances, the Internet and the resources it offers expand educational opportunities for motivated learners. He nonchalantly mentioned a new website he was using with his kids: the Khan Academy.

In a follow-up question, Gates emphasized the need to put more focus on education and the practices of great teachers than on Wall Street businessmen and financial analysts. Gates's greatest praise of Khan was that he had left a successful job in finance to pursue something much

When he praised the Khan Academy at the 2010 Aspen Ideas Festival, Microsoft cofounder Bill Gates gave Salman Khan an unexpected boost into the tech spotlight. He now famously said of Khan, "It was a good day his wife let him quit his job."

The Bill & Melinda Gates Foundation

Bill Gates is an American business magnate perhaps best known as the cofounder and former chief executive and chairman of the personal computer company Microsoft. Since stepping down from his role at the helm of Microsoft in 2000, Gates has become very well known as an investor and philanthropist, donating large portions of his and his wife Melinda's personal wealth to charitable causes.

In their capacity as two of the largest donors in American philanthropy, Gates and his wife founded the Bill & Melinda Gates Foundation in 2000. The husband-and-wife team are two of the three trustees, along with Warren Buffet, another wealthy American philanthropist and investor. The Gates Foundation provides funding to causes of high interest to Bill and Melinda Gates, often aimed at enhancing health care, reducing poverty, or expanding educational opportunities.

In October 2010, the Gates Foundation provided a grant in the amount of $1,464,667 to the Khan Academy, with the stated goal of expanding its leadership and staff capacity and helping map its content in line with the Common Core high school standards. Funding from grants from the Gates Foundation and similar groups have made it possible for Internet-based organizations such as the Khan Academy to grow and expand their impact.

As of September 2013, the Gates Foundation had an endowment of more than $40 billion, and it was providing annual grant payments in the amount of $3.4 billion. In addition to the Khan Academy, other programs to which the Gates Foundation has made charitable donations include the Global Fund to Fight AIDS, Tuberculosis and Malaria, an organization that disburses and covers expenses for methods of prevention and treatment of various deadly diseases; the Alliance for Financial Inclusion, which supports economic infrastructure in poor and developing nations; and several scholarship programs and institutions of higher learning in the United States.

more meaningful. He was famously quoted as saying, "I'd say we've moved about 160 IQ points from the hedge fund category to the teaching-many-people-in-a-leveraged-way category. It was a good day his wife let him quit his job." The mention and praise earned the Khan Academy an immediate surge in attention.

The praise and backing of Khan's decision reflects an important reality of many of the entrepreneurs who are changing the world with the tools offered by the Internet. This reality is that most of them are highly intelligent people who must sacrifice a well-laid-out career path for the sake of creating something bigger. While Khan was influenced by a waning economy at the time, his decision to leave his job as a financial analyst was more heavily weighted toward his desire to grow something unique out of the Khan Academy. He was essentially sacrificing a promising career that would earn him big bucks to go out on a limb with a new, unthought-of endeavor. He was able to channel his life experiences into an innovative project, and Gates expressed great admiration for this willingness and sacrifice.

Khan wasn't present at the Aspen Ideas Festival to hear Gates's speech, and before that point, he wasn't even aware that Gates knew who he was. His first big supporter, Ann Doerr, was the one who sent a series of text messages informing him of what Gates was saying—text messages that Khan couldn't believe until he searched Google and saw that it was true. Shortly after that, Gates reached out and brought Khan to his offices in Seattle, Washington, to present more information on the Khan Academy. The meeting was nerve-racking for Khan, but Gates was impressed.

"BILL GATES'S FAVORITE TEACHER"

Two days after Khan and Gates first met in Seattle, *Fortune* magazine published an exposé titled "Bill Gates' Favorite Teacher," and the philanthropic establishment quickly positioned itself behind the Khan Academy. Through the Gates Foundation, Bill Gates secured a $1.5 million grant for the Khan Academy for office space and to hire a small team. That grant was followed by another $4 million for other projects, including content creation. Around the same time, Google at last followed through on Khan's earlier proposal and awarded him the $2 million donation they had initially discussed.

Following their meeting, Gates did a brief feature about the Khan Academy on his online series, the *Gates Notes*, which covers ideas for reform in education, health care, energy, and other topics of interest to the American public. The *Gates Notes* feature repeatedly emphasized the one-person staff of the Khan Academy, as well as that Khan, acting alone, was able to use the Internet to create such an impactful educational model.

In the October 2010 *Gates Notes* video clip, Khan states, "I want [the Khan Academy] to be a standalone virtual school where anyone in the world who wants to learn anything can go there, start from the basics, progress as far as they need to go … and eventually I want it to

After the initial shout-out in Aspen, Gates went on to be a key supporter of Khan, with several million dollars in grants from his Gates Foundation earmarked for staff development, office space, and content creation.

actually become the operating system for what goes on in the classroom." With this expansive idea, Khan expressed his desire to implement a new learning model in which students could progress at their own pace, with the teacher serving as a mentor or tutor to help guide each student's academic development.

Big dreams often require big funding, and Gates's focus on the Khan Academy sought to do just that. Along with the donations from the Doerrs and Google, Khan now had more than enough resources to obtain an office space in which to work and record his videos, the ability to hire a small staff to develop the software and engineering, and the potential to expand the content available on the Khan Academy website—including translations into ten new languages.

It is important to note that, true to style, Khan did not see a need to complicate the academy's system once he had sufficient funding to create new elements. Instead, he kept the basic premise the same and simply expanded and improved upon the content already being offered. Later, the academy would venture into providing content and lessons on subject areas other than math, and voices other than Khan's were added to the mix. Yet the website always maintained the simple style of the original short video clips and customized exercise problems that Khan himself created for math. The Gates's seal of approval didn't change the Khan Academy's model; it simply helped it reach more people.

CHAPTER 5

Flipping the Classroom

Salman Khan's vision of turning his website into a global learning institution always seemed far-fetched. After all, in its early years, the Khan Academy lacked the funding and staff necessary to expand its content and software in the ways needed to become a standalone learning institution. Even through mid-2010, Khan remained the only employee of the academy, and he continued to operate out of a closet in his own home. It was Ann Doerr's donation that was the beginning of a change in tide for Khan.

A STANDALONE VIRTUAL SCHOOL

Within a few months, funding and attention from the Doerrs, Google, and the Gates Foundation gave Khan the means to begin to grow his academy and implement some of the changes he had envisioned. As delineated in his interview for the *Gates Notes* video feature, Khan had begun to

Khan's flipped-classroom model has been the focus of many a debate on educational reform. Here, Anant Agarwal (president of edX, a massive open online course platform on which unlimited students may simultaneously take a course), Khan, and Biddy Martin (president of Amherst College) debate educational reform together.

see his website as something more than just a substitute for a tutor. He wanted the Khan Academy to become "a stand-alone virtual school" offering a free, self-paced educational experience for anybody who so desired it.

Furthermore, Khan began to picture an inverted classroom model, a process he called "flipping the class-room." In traditional education models, students gather in classes to learn new content together with a single teacher. Afterward, each individual goes home, does practice problems for homework, and attempts to reinforce the ideas on his or her own. If somebody isn't grasping a concept or requires additional explanation and reinforcement, the review becomes a class activity the next day, given that there is only one teacher and many students. This was Khan's experience of the school system throughout his youth.

In Khan's "flipped" classroom, learning new material would occur from videos, with each student having access to a computer to learn materials at his or her own rate. Each person in a classroom could theoretically progress as quickly or slowly as needed to maintain interest but could also thoroughly review content by rewinding and pausing the videos. The teacher would be reserved to act as a hands-on tutor, moving from student to student to help explain more difficult concepts.

The idea stemmed from feedback that Khan received from teachers regarding the Khan Academy. In *The One World Schoolhouse*, Khan says, "Some [teachers] were pointing their students to the videos as a supplemental tool. Others, however, were using them to rethink their classrooms altogether." In the latter group, the teachers were utilizing class time to perform problem-solving exercises that were usually sent home with a student at the end of the day as homework.

For Khan, this idea created the maximum benefit out of the academy. Instead of boring students with a passive fifty-minute lecture in class and then leaving kids to put

Jack Parker watches a video on the U.S. electoral system at home on his own time. The Khan Academy flipped-classroom model promotes learning content from the web modules at home and using class time to practice exercises and reinforce learning.

the ideas into practice without support at home, these teachers let the learning occur in Khan's ten- to fifteen-minute videos in the students' free time, going on to utilize collective time to work on exercises and address problems as they arose.

Additionally, learning at home proved to be a more independent and on-demand model. Rather than risk embarrassment in front of a group of peers by asking a question, somebody struggling with a concept could simply rewatch, rewind, and pause the material at his

The Digital Learning Boom

Before the Khan Academy existed, there were, in fact, other initiatives to increase digital learning and the use of technology inside (and outside of) the classroom. Computers have been used on school and university campuses dating back to the 1970s, when Apple frequently donated early-model computers to colleges. An August 1977 article in the Eureka, California, newspaper the *Times Standard* titled "Computers Breathing Down on Our Education" estimated that approximately two million students between kindergarten and twelfth grade were using computers annually at that time. Nonetheless, in the early days of computers in the classroom, the computer-to-student ratio was exceptionally low.

In the 1980s and 1990s, computer education and the presence of computer labs in schools became increasingly commonplace. In 1989, the University of Phoenix launched an online-learning program targeting working adults who desired a college diploma. The school's peak enrollment in 2010 was six hundred thousand students, although low graduation rates and the high cost of the courses have led to a consistent and steep decline in enrollment since then.

The program that perhaps comes closest to the Khan Academy's format is iTunes U, a digital learning program that makes use of Apple's iTunes digital media store infrastructure to distribute lessons online. Launched exclusively for college-level students in 2007, iTunes U initially allowed educators to assign, distribute, and even upload learning modules to accompany their classroom curriculums. By 2008, the program was expanded to include content targeting elementary, middle, and high school students. While iTunes U is a free service like the Khan Academy, it neither provides exercises nor the tools and data to track student progress. By providing that service, the Khan Academy has in many ways fulfilled the early vision of computers in the classroom.

iTunes U is just one of the digital learning platforms that have taken center stage as computers become increasingly integrated into classrooms. While it is free, iTunes U does not provide exercises or track user progress.

or her own speed. Class time would be used to reinforce the concepts and focus on the specific problems students found difficult.

Khan acknowledges that this concept certainly existed before the Khan Academy, but he felt that his video database and the Internet provided an opportunity to truly put it into practice. Indeed, with the popularity of the academy and its new endorsements and big-name investors, "flipping the classroom" became an attainable idea and Khan was quick to find school districts willing to implement it.

THE LOS ALTOS SCHOOL DISTRICT

As Khan developed a broader idea of how to use the Khan Academy as an integral part of the education system, rather than simply as an after-school tutorial or supplement to classroom learning and homework, opportunities opened for him to implement his new idea. In late 2010, that pivotal year for Khan, his academy began a pilot program with three teachers and 120 students in the Los Altos school district in Santa Clara County, California. Initial results were promising. By fall 2011, the program was implemented across all classrooms in grades five through six, as well as some seventh- and eighth-grade classrooms, too, with fifty teachers and over a thousand students involved.

For the program, teachers used mobile labs to supplement their standard curriculums. In mobile labs, students focused on the mathematical concepts they found challenging or difficult, with each student given the freedom to focus on the topics with which he or she struggled the most. Teachers used the data and measurements of progress on the website to plan more creative activities to reinforce those concepts that students seemed to grapple with the most.

The superintendent of the school district, Jeff Baier, publicized that the goal of the program was to make learning meaningful for each student. In his eyes, the Khan Academy could be used as a resource to provide the right types of lessons in the right presentation and at the right time for each pupil in the school district. That type of individualized learning was extremely beneficial and seemed to work on various levels.

In addition to the benefits of the program for students, Baier saw an impact on the instructors' use of time. The real-time tracking of each user's progress on the academy allowed teachers to more closely follow their classrooms' progressions. Teachers also found that they had more time and could more easily adjust their focus, avoiding large chunks of time spent on concepts that students seemed to easily grasp and dedicating more focus to difficult modules on which underperformance was noted.

Perhaps most important, students became significantly more enthused about their learning process. One of the sixth-grade teachers, Kami Thordarson, reported that her students raved for weeks about how great the program was, while other teachers noted increased freedom in their classroom approaches. Struggling students could be pulled aside in smaller groups to reinforce concepts, while other students could continue to be engaged with new modules and more advanced information at the same time. Lessons could be geared directly for each student depending on the precise problems that he or she answered incorrectly on the Khan Academy exercises.

The success of the program in the Los Altos school district made Khan believe that he, indeed, could finally revolutionize learning. One consequence of the program was certainly a growing debate on the usefulness of existing curriculums and the benefits of trying new approaches.

REINVENTING EDUCATION

As Khan explored ways to implement his "flipped classroom" ideal, the initial success in schools such as those in the Los Altos school district encouraged him to keep promoting the use of the Khan Academy in traditional classrooms—not just as a supplement to learning but as a more integral part of it. He began to envision new ways to use the academy and the impact it could truly have on education. To that effect, Khan gave a TED Talk in March 2011 on the use of video to rethink approaches to traditional education. The talk is titled "Let's Use Video to Reinvent Education."

By that point, there were already 2,200 videos offered on the Khan Academy website and more than one million users logging on each month. Furthermore, the pilot program in the Los Altos school district was going strong. The TED Talk was a great opportunity to express the ideas that Khan was beginning to develop after the influx of financial support and attention the academy received throughout 2010.

In the twenty-minute video, Khan reviewed his early motivation to develop the Khan Academy and discussed some of the earliest YouTube comments he had received. Among them were remarks from teachers who were, indeed, "flipping" their classrooms, assigning Khan Academy video-lectures to be watched by their students at home and then using classroom time to solve practice problems that had previously been reserved for homework.

In his TED Talk, Khan used the same laid-back, friendly tone that had come to define the Khan Academy videos, despite standing before a large crowd of Silicon Valley–based investors and adults instead of his usual target audience: elementary, middle, and high school students. Just as he was accustomed to doing in the videos on the website, Khan used his trademark disarming demeanor to break down the brilliant—and paradoxical—impact of the use of videos in education.

TED Talks

TED (an acronym that stands for "technology," "entertainment," and "design") is a nonprofit organization that hosts conferences on innovative ideas and promotes open discussion, collaboration, and exchange of thoughts. It started out as a onetime conference planned by the architect and graphic designer Richard Saul Wurman in 1984. Wurman sought to converge the three fields that became the namesake of TED: technology, entertainment, and design. At the 1984 TED conference, Sony displayed a demo of what would become the compact disc, and Apple showed its Macintosh computer for the first time.

In 1990, TED conferences became an annual occurrence in Long Beach, California. Over the next two decades, TED developed additional projects, including TEDGlobal, which promotes conferences and discussions in countries other than the United States, and TED Fellows, which creates a community of young innovative thinkers by providing a platform for the exchange of ideas. One of TED's best-known projects is TED.com, its website where Internet users may watch more than 1,500 recorded TED Talks for free.

Many renowned and popular figures have given TED Talks, including former U.S. president

Bill Clinton, British anthropologist Jane Goodall, and cofounder of Apple Steve Jobs. Given the creative ideas they present and the high-profile names featured, TED Talks have become an increasingly popular part of global culture. Salman Khan gave his lecture "Let's Use Video to Reinvent Education" at TED 2011, and by early 2014, the video had received more than three million views.

British anthropologist Jane Goodall is well known for her study of primates, specifically chimpanzees. In 2007 and 2008, she gave two TED Talks that focused on the relationship between humans and animals.

Khan explained that through the employ of videos to provide lectures, "these teachers have used technology to humanize the classroom." Class time had become an engaging experience in which students interacted with each other and their teacher. It also removed what Khan deems the "one-size-fits-all" education model, wherein every student in a classroom must learn at the same rate. In turn, each individual can move through practice problems, repeat them, and review them at his or her own speed.

Khan likened use of the Khan Academy to riding a bike. No matter how many times an adult explains how to ride a bike to a young child, it is only through the experience of riding, falling, and attempting to ride again that he or she will learn to maintain the right mix of balance and speed in order to succeed. Likewise, explaining math to a group of students and then leaving them to practice the theories on their own time is not as effective as letting them learn the procedures in shorter, more engaging videos at home and then dedicating class time to games, problem solving, and real applications.

Khan also showed examples of teacher dashboards from the Los Altos school district pilot program and explained how using data on their students' performance across a variety of modules on the Khan Academy website was allowing these educators to focus their attention primarily on problem areas and those students who were lagging on a certain concept at any given time, rather than trying to address all students on the same topic simultaneously.

A GLOBAL, ONE-WORLD CLASSROOM

At the end of his TED Talk, Khan had a question-and-answer session with his biggest supporter to date, Bill Gates, where many of the questions addressed the Los Altos pilot program. One of the most telling questions Gates posed was, "Is this ready for primetime? Do you think a lot of classes next school year should try this thing out?" Khan's answer was indicative of the plans he would unravel over the next few years.

He insisted that with the traffic the site had already received up until that point, coupled with the positive impact demonstrated in the pilot program, there was no reason why the academy couldn't be used in every school district in the country starting the very next day. The constantly evolving software and feedback from staff and students meant that the data offered by the Khan Academy and dashboards could be adjusted as desired for each classroom's needs. Gates's final words were "I think you just got a glimpse of the future of education," and indeed, Khan went on to develop more wide-spread implementation plans.

OAKLAND UNITY HIGH SCHOOL

Oakland Unity High School (OUHS) is a charter school in Oakland, California, that started its own pilot program with the Khan Academy in fall 2011. Unlike the program in the Los Altos school district, the high school students at OUHS had a learning lab four days a week, outside of standard class time. The purpose was to bring incoming ninth-grade students who had tested below level in algebra up to par.

Instructors, in turn, met weekly to coordinate their curriculums and make sure that they stayed in line with the subject areas students were practicing on the Khan academy website. In this way, they were able to integrate the academy into their teaching as a means of filling in areas of knowledge that certain students lacked and concentrating class time on the topics with which students struggled the most.

In the first three years of the program, OUHS average scores on California standardized mathematics tests consistently improved. In 2010, the year before the program began, the school tested with an average score of 281, ranking 1,078 out of 1,340 public high schools in the state. By 2013, OUHS had an average score of 384 across ninth-graders and ranked eleventh out of schools statewide.

SUMMIT PUBLIC SCHOOLS

Probably one of the more interesting case studies of how the Khan Academy can effect great changes in public education is in the Summit charter school network in the Bay

Area surrounding San Francisco, California. For the 2011–2012 school year, two of the Summit charter schools in San Jose piloted a Khan Academy program with almost two hundred ninth-graders. Classes were divided into thirty-five students, with each student assigned a computer.

So far, this sounds like a familiar Khan Academy story. After all, both of the programs already discussed

Teacher Jesse Roe of the Summit charter school in San Jose, California, uses Khan Academy videos and software as integrated parts of his curriculum.

involved new, self-paced curriculums where students learned at their own rate via the academy modules. Year two of the Summit program is where things became particularly interesting.

For the 2012–2013 school year, the schools took on a blended-learning approach. Two hundred students were combined into one collective class, with seven teachers circulating among the students. These seven educators became face-to-face, individualized tutors who managed small groups, workshops, and labs. The schools also eliminated traditional grade levels, instead grouping students into three categories: High School Ready, College Ready, and Early College.

This seemingly radical approach is actually a relatively simple way to implement the Khan Academy into a public school and free up the rigid ways in which students often learn. By addressing their classes' specific needs and allowing progression at a personalized pace, these educators have seen improvements in learning, focus, and test scores. The Summit schools program became another Khan Academy success story.

EXPANSION INTO MORE SCHOOLS

Khan's vision of the academy becoming a "global, one-world classroom" derives from his belief that when the same content covering every topic taught in schools is available on one free website, then educators, students, and adults who may have forgotten or never learned certain concepts can collaborate and learn together online. In turn, Khan envisions a global community of learners whose feedback could influence each other and the way education occurs in radical ways.

In addition to the programs in the Los Altos school district and Oakland Unity High School, Khan Academy pilots have been rolled out worldwide, including another pilot program spanning forty-eight schools in Idaho; a training and implementation program impacting eleven Innova schools in Lima, Peru; and even a pilot involving 460 fifth-graders, their parents, and teachers at the Center for Reading and Cultural Activities in Yaoundé, the capital of the African nation of Cameroon.

The Khan Academy maintains a blog (http://schools.khanacademy.org) where these global collaborators are able to share their stories and experiences, as well as the benefits and disadvantages that they have seen in their use of the Khan Academy. In this way, Khan's vision of a global, one-world classroom shows promise of becoming a practical reality.

Despite all the success stories, the growing media attention to the Khan Academy has had two effects that continue to be observed today. On the one hand, the extensive praise and hype has turned Salman Khan into a highly influential popular figure, with a large following in the fields of technology and education, making him somewhat of a cultural celebrity.

On the other hand, there are still vast roadblocks to Khan's vision of a global, one-world classroom, and criticisms of the academy's teaching methodology persist. The last section of this title seeks to address both Khan's growing star power as an individual and the new challenges the Khan Academy has come to face.

CHAPTER 6

Collaborative Thinking and New Frontiers

The steady expansion of the Khan Academy's pilot programs in different school environments and the increasing variety in video content offered on the academy website helped bring the academy through the 2011–2012 school year. Then, in April 2012, Salman Khan made *Time* magazine's list of "The World's 100 Most Influential People."

With countless interviews, lectures, and consistent media publicity about the newest, most eye-catching programs being developed by the academy, Khan had become something of a celebrity in popular culture among educators, techies, and young adults. With this increase in visibility, Khan was able to make a shift from simply being the "cool tutor who makes videos" to becoming a notable advocate for education reform.

By 2012, persistent media hype and the growing number of school districts integrating the Khan Academy into their classrooms had made Salman Khan a recognizable figure both in the tech sphere and in the world of education.

THE KHAN ACADEMY DISCOVERY LAB

One of the new endeavors that the Khan Academy decided to try in summer 2012 was a series of three two-week, offline camps dubbed Discovery Labs. Each Discovery Lab ran six hours a day for over two weeks in Palo Alto, California. The Discovery Lab saw middle school students come together to engage in offline activities—projects such as robot building, taking apart common household electronics, and even making bets based on probability in a simulated casino.

For Khan, the summer camp was far more than just a camp. As many educators had criticized Khan's lack of training as a teacher in the early days of the Khan Academy, the Discovery Lab was a way for him to become more actively involved in observing *how* students learn. Face-to-face interaction had proven to be an important part of Khan's flipped-classroom model, so the Discovery Lab gave him the opportunity to observe that essential element to his plans for a new type of school.

Minli Virdone, one of the deans of the Discovery Lab, explained in a video on the academy's website, "At Khan Academy we felt that we needed our own version of the summer camp because we had so many ideas that we wanted to test out." By watching students engage in activities and observing the strengths and weaknesses of each idea, the Khan Academy was able to develop new, interesting content and better curriculums for its school programs.

The Discovery Lab program was a success. The Khan Academy repeated the program in 2013 and again learned a great deal from its observation of students in an interactive setting. While these offline summer camps may have seemed a little offbeat for the self-purported *digital* learning school, they pointed toward one of Khan's greater goals: to create a standalone, physical school based on the teaching methodology of the "flipped" classroom.

THE ONE-WORLD SCHOOLHOUSE

As founder of the Khan Academy, a husband and father, Bill Gates's favorite teacher, and now a summer camp director, Salman Khan took a next step that may have seemed unexpected for some. For him, however, it was the next logical platform to express his plans for education reform. In September 2012, British publishing house Hodder & Stoughton released *The One World Schoolhouse: Education Reimagined*, an e-book in which Khan explains the background of the Khan Academy, his own observations of public education from his youth, and practical changes that could lead to his ultimate goal: a free, world-class education for anybody on the planet.

The book's final chapter is dedicated to practical changes to improve education systems, and in it Khan delineates many of the practices with which the Khan Academy pilot programs in schools around the world have come to thrive. He espouses larger classrooms with teams of teachers rotating among students, combining students of various grades, and allowing each one to advance at his or her own rate. He even talks of doing away with summer vacations, instead promoting a plan similar to the adult working world in which each student would be able to take vacation whenever his or her family has planned a trip. This would avoid a three-month learning gap each year and also wouldn't be so problematic, as each student is already progressing at his or her own pace.

Another change Khan lays out in the book is eliminating the grading system. Just as the Khan Academy rewards persistence and success with badges but does not assign negative grades, Khan's ideal school would have only a passing grade because each student would continue to work at a single topic until achieving mastery over it. He also suggests an overhaul of the standardized testing system. Just imagine school without all of your merits being judged consistently on the basis of test scores. Khan would get rid of the report card and issue "creative portfolios."

All of the transformations that Khan would implement in his ideal school came from his practical observations of what did and didn't work in the Khan Academy pilot programs. While for many, these ideas were revolutionary or unsettling, for Khan they seemed like obvious solutions to many of the problems in the ways that schools instruct.

The most significant criticism of the book's advocacy, however, was its failure to address some of the grander structural problems in the education system. While Khan had done much work since the earliest days of the Khan Academy to study teaching and learning—the previously mentioned field called pedagogy—he failed to address school administration, funding for education, or many of the other problems that plague public school systems in countries such as the United States. After the release of the book (as an e-book in 2012, followed by a paperback edition in late 2013), Khan would have to go on to face many of the practical roadblocks to his vision for the Khan Academy.

PARTNERSHIPS AND COLLABORATIONS

A vision as big as Khan's requires a substantial team and a network of like-minded people who can help develop and expand it in every area necessary. The year 2012 was the beginning of a period of exciting new partnerships and collaborations for the Khan Academy, ones that would help it develop even better, more diverse content and spread that content to new places previously not thought possible.

One noteworthy new collaborator was Craig Silverstein. In 1998, Silverstein had been Google's first employee, number three in the company after Google's cofounders. Silverstein had followed Google from its infancy in dorm rooms at Stanford University to the technological power-house that it had become just over a decade later. In early 2012, Silverstein left Google to become a developer for the Khan Academy.

Another high-profile collaboration that came later in 2012 was with National Basketball Association (NBA) star LeBron James. In a series of videos titled "LeBron Asks," the basketball star asks questions on probability, such as the odds of making a certain number of consecutive free throws, and Khan explains the answer.

According to a quote from Khan featured in an *ESPN Playbook* article in December 2012, James's motivation was altruistic, claiming, "If Michael Jordan told me and my friends to study harder, we would have, so I'm going to tell kids to study harder." The collaboration was just another of Khan Academy's efforts to reach new audi-ences. It inspired Khan to think bigger and solicit help from other sports stars and organizations, including the race-car driving association NASCAR and players from the National Football League (NFL).

Other collaborations in 2012–13 were fueled less by big names and more predominantly sought to involve bright young people. A new series of videos produced in conjunction with the MIT's MIT + K12 program led to MIT + Khan Academy. MIT + K12 is a website that hosts

Featuring popular celebrities, such as LeBron James in the "LeBron Asks" series, has allowed the Khan Academy to reach new audiences and make topics such as probability fun and engaging. Here, a cartoon LeBron takes a shot!

videos created by MIT students on a variety of STEM topics. The new collaboration benefited both parties. On the one hand, it provided new video content for the Khan academy, and on the other hand, it gave MIT + K12 the already established network of viewers and users that the academy had, expanding the videos' reach.

Another young partner for the Khan Academy was Vi Hart, who joined the team in early 2013. Hart had gained popularity as a "mathemusician," creating entertaining

The Khan Academy's expansion into non-STEM subject areas has produced new, fascinating content. Examples, such as those seen here in an e-mail to subscribers, include links to a tour of ancient Rome, as well as to whether or not whales have lice.

videos on YouTube about various topics in mathematics. Similar to Khan's own early videos, Hart's pieces featured "doodling" and a laid-back, second-person narration. These YouTube videos went viral, garnering millions of views and bringing Hart to Khan's attention.

Each of these partnerships fulfills the Khan Academy's goal of tapping into new areas of knowledge, creative twists on its classic format, and the ultimate ambition: hosting a world-class free education.

REACHING NEW FRONTIERS

To date, the most practical challenge the Khan Academy has faced is that, despite having a well-designed and constantly evolving website, having managed to obtain substantial funding from big-name donors and organizations, and having developed effective means for implementing the academy as an educational supplement in pilot programs around the world as part of its "flipped" classroom model, there are still regions and schools where Internet access is limited by cost and underdeveloped infrastructure.

Beginning in 2012, Salman Khan, being the visionary that he has always proven to be, began to spend his time seeking solutions to the academy's major dilemma. One of the solutions he came up with is KA Lite. KA Lite is open-source software that may be downloaded onto any computer, allowing users to view and interact with Khan Academy lectures and exercises that have been downloaded in advance.

KA Lite allows students to connect to and use the academy's tools even when there is no Internet access by connecting to a central server. When Internet is available, the data stored in KA Lite can be synced back to a central server, providing the similar progress and experience that online Khan Academy users have. Video and content are distributed through BitTorrent, a program that allows users to share videos they've downloaded, as well as download new videos simultaneously from other users.

In certain rural areas, such as villages in the western and eastern cape of South Africa, an entire school shares a single, slow Internet connection. With KA Lite, such schools can use the Khan Academy content and methodology without the expensive installation of multiple Internet connections to allow each student to work online. By working individually and synchronizing with the central server, which in turn connects to the Internet to sync, countless students can benefit from the academy tools offline.

Another major effort to reach new audiences is a groundbreaking deal that the Khan Academy announced with cable and Internet service provider Comcast in December 2013. While the academy has won over huge followings in those schools privileged enough to afford multiple computers per classroom, as well as the wide-reaching "tech" world, many lower-income families are not aware of its services or the opportunities it offers. In addition to a substantial cash donation to the academy, Comcast announced it would donate hundreds of thousands of public service ads for the academy. The goal is to make the Khan Academy a household name outside of the tech sphere. Furthermore, the Khan Academy website will be featured as a prominent learning portal on Comcast's Internet Essentials service, which provides

BitTorrent

BitTorrent is an Internet protocol, or digital system of data exchange, that supports peer-to-peer file sharing primarily geared toward distributing very large files. A torrent file is a computer file containing metadata about which files or folders should be distributed to other Internet users. It links to a larger file and manages the simultaneous download of different portions of that file from a variety of users.

In practice, BitTorrent allows a single user to upload a large file, such as a video, as what becomes known as the "seed." That user then distributes a torrent file to other users. The torrent file connects those additional users to the original seed file, and these users, in turn, become known as "leechers," or downloaders of the original file. The benefit of BitTorrent is that it allows users to simultaneously download and upload parts of the same file, reducing use of Internet traffic and helping maintain relatively quicker download speeds. The most widely used BitTorrent software is a program called μTorrent. By early 2012, there were at least 150 million active users of μTorrent, and that number has steadily increased since then.

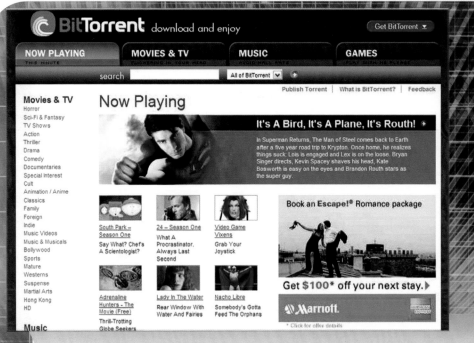

BitTorrent has proven controversial for its role in the distribution of pirated movies, TV shows, and music. Some, however, see benefits in its ability to mass distribute large files. In 2012, the Khan Academy used it to create KA Lite for users with slow or limited Internet access.

Despite the benefits it offers, BitTorrent has been a controversial protocol. It is widely used to share pirated material such as popular movies, albums, and other works of copyright-protected art that would otherwise be too large a file to easily transfer online. Since 2005, there has been a steady increase in legal action in the United States to shut down popular BitTorrent websites that distribute torrent files, as well as charges raised against the founders and operators of said sites.

(continued on the next page)

(continued from the previous page)

Nonetheless, many see practical benefits in the ability to mass-distribute large files over BitTorrent software. The Khan Academy's offline program KA Lite, for example, uses torrent files to distribute the large video tutorials from the academy website, as well as exercises and other files to regions where poor infrastructure or cost prohibit widespread or high-speed Internet access. As a result, schools in these areas can download the necessary content to a central server and connect to other computers on their network that don't have direct or fast Internet access and redistribute the free files.

low-cost Internet access to many who cannot afford faster broadband service.

CONCLUSION

Developments such as KA Lite and the Khan Academy-Comcast partnership demonstrate Salman Khan's continued devotion to his earliest goal: that no person should be denied a free, top-quality education. Salman Khan has consistently proven his dedication to his cause, whether through the classic Khan Academy model of online, engaging tutoring modules; the "flipped" classroom curriculum, which sees the academy's exercises featured prominently during school hours with a teacher who acts as a coach and its video content assigned as homework; hours spent doodling on Yahoo! Messenger with a cousin; or exciting probability videos shot with LeBron James.

From the first tutoring sessions with his cousin Nadia, Khan has witnessed flaws in an educational system that few dared to challenge. He has also used creative ideas and the best tools the Internet has to offer to get around those roadblocks. As the academy grew and overcame its significant initial challenges with funding, software development, and even finding the most successful teaching methodology, it has come to face even greater challenges to the one-world, global classroom. But just as he always has, Khan continues to look for innovative ways to get his school out to the people.

At the beginning of this profile, you imagined your typical school day: a strict routine, long lectures, and frustrating homework. Now with tools such as the Khan Academy, you can rethink education in an entirely different way. After all, that's exactly what Salman Khan did, and it's created an educational revolution.

Fact Sheet on

SALMAN KHAN

Full name: Salman "Sal" Amin Khan

Date of birth: October 11, 1976

Hometown: New Orleans, Louisiana

Current residence: Mountain View, California

Ethnicity: Bengali-American

Spouse: Umaima Marvi

Children: Huzaifa Khan, son
       Manahil Khan, daughter

Elementary School: Phoebe Hearst Elementary School Metairie, Louisiana

High School: Grace King High School Metairie, Louisiana

Undergraduate Degrees: Bachelor of science (BS) in mathematics, Massachusetts Institute of Technology (MIT), 1998

BS in electrical engineering and computer science, MIT, 1998

Master of engineering (MEng) in electrical engineering and computer science, MIT, 1998

Graduate Degree: Master of business administration (MBA) degree, Harvard University, 2003

First job: Hedge fund analyst at Wohl Capital Management

Current position: Executive director of the Khan Academy

Fact Sheet on

KHAN ACADEMY

Founder: Salman Khan

Executive Director: Salman Khan

President: Shantanu Sinha

COO (Chief operating officer): Shantanu Sinha

Full-time employees: 50

Part-time collaborators and volunteers: 34

Content specialists: 26

Date founded: September 2006

Headquarters: Mountain View, California

Languages offered: Arabic, Armenian, Bengali, Bulgarian, Chinese (Mandarin), Czech, Danish, Dutch, English, French, German, Greek, Hebrew, Indonesian, Italian, Norwegian, Persian, Polish, Portuguese (Brazil), Portuguese (Portugal), Russian, Spanish, Swahili, Telugu, Thai, Turkish, Ukrainian, Urdu, and Xhosa

Number of English-language YouTube videos: Over 5,000 (as of February 2014)

Number of YouTube subscribers: Over 1.5 million (as of February 2014)

Number of YouTube page views: Over 350 million (as of February 2014)

Number of unique users per month: Approximately 10 million (as of November 2013)

Number of practice problems completed daily: Approximately 4 million (as of November 2013)

Number of practice problems available: Over 100,000 (as of November 2013)

Number of classrooms using the Khan Academy: Approximately 30,000 (as of February 2014)

Timeline

October 11, 1976 Salman Khan is born in New Orleans, Louisiana.

1994 Khan graduates from Grace King High School as valedictorian.

1994 Khan begins college at the Massachusetts Institute of Technology (MIT).

1997–1998 Khan is his class president at MIT.

1998 Khan graduates with three separate degrees (a bachelor of science [BS] in mathematics, another BS in electrical engineering and computer science, as well as a master of engineering (MEng) in electrical engineering and computer science) from MIT.

2001 Khan begins graduate school at the Harvard Business School.

June–August 2002 Khan works briefly at a tech research company called Parc.

2003 Khan receives a master of business administration (MBA) degree from Harvard.

May 2003 Khan begins to work as an analyst at Wohl Capital Management.

August 2004 Khan begins to remotely tutor his younger cousin Nadia via Yahoo! Doodle.

November 16, 2006 The Khan Academy channel is started on YouTube so that multiple cousins and family friends can watch Khan's videos on their own time.

2008 The Khan Academy is incorporated as a 501c(3) nonprofit organization.

April 2008 Khan leaves his job as a senior analyst at Wohl Capital Management.

2009 Khan and his wife Umaima's first child, a son named Huzaifa, is born.

2009 Khan briefly works another financial analyst job at Connective Capital Management, LLC, before definitively leaving that career.

2009 The Khan Academy receives the Microsoft Tech Award for Education.

January 2010 Google invites Salman Khan to make a presentation and proposal for a grant.

Early 2010 Approximately 200,000 people are logging on to the Khan Academy website each month. Ann Doerr writes a donation to Khan and suggests the two meet up. After meeting, she offers another $100,000 donation.

July 5–11, 2010 The annual Aspen Ideas Festival takes place. In his interview session, Bill Gates praises Salman Khan and the Khan Academy, causing a media frenzy.

Timeline

September 2010 The Khan Academy receives a $1.5 million grant from the Bill & Melinda Gates Foundation, as well as a $2 million grant from Google to expand staff and language support.

October 2010 Salman Khan is featured on *Fortune* magazine's annual "40 under 40" list.

Fall 2010 The Khan Academy begins a pilot program in the Los Altos school district in Santa Clara County, California.

March 2011 Khan gives a TED talk titled "Let's Use Video to Reinvent Education."

Mid-2011 Khan and his wife have a second child, a daughter named Manahil.

Fall 2011 The Los Altos school district program expands across all classrooms in grades five and six, as well as some seventh- and eighth-grade classrooms. Oakland Unity High School and two Summit charter schools also start their own pilot programs using the Khan Academy.

April 2012 Salman Khan is included on *Time* magazine's list of "The World's 100 Most Influential People."

Late Spring 2012 Khan is the guest speaker at both Rice University and MIT's commencement ceremonies.

June 2012 Two teachers create a popular video pointing out each mistake that occurs in a Khan Academy video, drawing focus to flaws in the academy's approach to teaching.

Summer 2012 The Khan Academy launches its summer Discovery Lab program.

Fall 2012 The Summit charter school program enacts a blended learning approach, combining two hundred students into a single classroom, each working with the Khan Academy at an individual pace.

September 2012 Khan's first book, *The One World Schoolhouse: Education Reimagined*, is released online.

May 2013 Khan is the guest speaker at the University of New Orleans' commencement ceremony.

December 2013 U.S. media giant Comcast announces a partnership with the Khan Academy to provide free advertising for its services and inclusion in its low-cost Internet Essentials package.

March 2014 The College Board and the Khan Academy announce their partnership in which the academy will provide free test preparation for the redesigned SAT.

Glossary

advocate A person who argues for, recommends, or supports a cause or policy.

broadcast lecture A talk given before an audience or class, especially for instruction in which one professor addresses many students.

conceptual Of, relating to, or consisting of knowledge of general ideas.

customized Built, fit, or changed to suit a specific customer.

dashboard A page at the front of the control panel used to manage a website.

disarming Tending to remove any feelings of unfriendliness or distrust.

exposé A report or formal statement of facts.

flipped classroom A learning model in which students learn new content online at home (predominantly through videos) and solve problems and exercises in class with a teacher.

grant A gift (as of money or land) for a particular purpose.

hedge fund A group of investors who take financial risks together in order to try to earn a lot of money.

infrastructure The underlying foundation or basic framework (as of a system or organization).

instant message A system for sending messages quickly over the Internet from one computer or cell phone to another computer or cell phone.

JavaScript A dynamic computer programming language designed to communicate instructions to a computer.

least common multiple The smallest number that two numbers both divide into evenly.

leecher In BitTorrent, a user who downloads a large file through a torrent.

mathlete A person who competes in mathematics competitions.

metadata Data that provides an informational overview of other data.

module An educational unit that covers a single subject or topic.

MOOC A massive open online course, a type of online learning platform in which a theoretically unlimited number of students can simultaneously watch and participate in the same class.

pedagogy The art, science, or profession of teaching.

philanthropist A person who performs charitable acts or gives gifts.

pretest A test to find out if students are prepared for further studies.

procedural Relating to or comprising memory or knowledge concerned with how to manipulate symbols, concepts, and rules to accomplish a task or solve a problem.

protocol A digital system of data exchange.

real time The actual time during which something takes place.

reform The improvement of something by removing or correcting faults, problems, etc.

screenshot An image that shows the contents of a computer display.

seed A machine possessing the complete file from which other users may download that file via a torrent.

software The programs and related information used by a computer.

standardized testing A means of providing a set of questions or problems in which every person taking the test is given the exact same test under the same exact conditions.

STEM An acronym that stands for the fields of study of science, technology, engineering, and mathematics as a collective.

supplemental Additional.

synchronize To cause to agree in time.

tablet A device by which pictures, graphs, or maps are put into a computer in a manner similar to drawing.

top-heavy fraction An improper fraction, or a fraction in which the top number (numerator) is larger than or equal to the bottom number (denominator).

torrent A type of file that contains instructions in the form of metadata about other files to be downloaded or distributed.

traffic The amount of data transmitted by visitors to a website.

venture capitalist Someone who invests capital (as retained corporate earnings or individual savings) or makes capital available for investment in the ownership element of a new or fresh enterprise.

Canada Science and Technology Museum
P.O. Box 9724, Station T
Ottawa, ON K1G 5A3
Canada
(866) 442-4416
Website: http://www.sciencetech.technomuses.ca
The Canada Science and Technology Museum is the
largest STEM-based museum in Canada, with a
special focus on the role that science and technology have played in Canadian society. Public
programming and activities geared toward schools
and students make the museum an important cor-
nerstone of science education in Canada.

Center for Education Reform (CER)
910 Seventeenth Street NW, 11th Floor
Washington, DC 20006
(800) 521-2118
Website: http://www.edreform.com
The CER is an organization dedicated to developing sus-
tainable and structural changes to education policy
with the goal of increasing and improving learning

possibilities in the long term. A major focus of the CER is digital learning and the means of implementing digital literacy into classroom curriculums.

CODE
321 Chapel Street
Ottawa, ON K1N 7Z2
Canada
(800) 661-2633
Website: http://www.codecan.org
CODE is one of the leading nongovernmental organizations in Canada dedicated to promoting literacy and education reform. CODE's efforts to support libraries, schools, and educational development make it a great resource for tools and information on education systems worldwide.

Digital Media Academy (DMA)
718 University Avenue, Suite 115
Los Gatos, CA 95032
(866) 656-3342
Website: http://www.digitalmediaacademy.org
Founded at Stanford University in 2002, the DMA offers summer camps and continuing education courses for young students and adults alike in the core STEM subject areas. With a focus on using digital tools to approach science, technology, engineering, and

mathematics, the DMA seeks to promote innovation and creation.

Emagination Computer Camps
54 Stiles Road, Suite 205
Salem, NH 03079
(877) 248-0206
Website: http://www.computercamps.com
Emagination Computer Camps is a nationwide, accredited camp organization dedicated to teaching and engaging teens interested in technology and computers. Its tech programs and workshops provide the digital tools necessary to be an advanced learner, both in and out of the classroom.

iD Tech
910 E. Hamilton Avenue, Suite 300
Campbell, CA 95008
(888) 709-TECH (8324)
Website: http://www.idtech.com
With roots as a small technology education camp run out of a garage, iD Tech has grown to become one of the largest nationwide camps specializing in STEM education for learners of all grades. Its online courses, year-round camps, and summer programs at top American universities make iD Tech an accessible option for young techies all over.

International Society for Technology in Education (ISTE)
1710 Rhode Island Avenue NW, Suite 900
Washington, DC 20036
(866) 654-4777
Website: https://www.iste.org
The ISTE is a nonprofit organization that promotes the
use of technology as a tool in education, as well as
the implementation of curricular uses of educational
technology. It promotes standards for both students
and teachers to create a more connected learning
experience through digital tools.

Khan Academy
P.O. Box 1630
Mountain View, CA 94042
Website: https://www.khanacademy.org
The Khan Academy is the premiere organization for
providing a world-class education free of cost to
anyone who seeks it. Through its online tutorials,
YouTube videos, and partnerships with schools
globally, the academy is a great resource for active,
engaged learners to push their boundaries.

National Center for Technological Literacy (NCTL)
Museum of Science, Boston
1 Science Park
Boston, MA 02114

(617) 723-2500

Website: http://legacy.mos.org/nctl

The NCTL is an initiative of the Museum of Science, Boston, which aims to develop and promote tech education programs in schools across the United States. With its curricular focus on STEM subject areas, the NCTL aims to give students a competitive edge and advanced knowledge of subject areas that will shape future technology.

WEBSITES

Because of the changing nature of Internet links, Rosen Publishing has developed an online list of websites related to the subject of this book. This site is updated regularly. Please use this link to access the list:

http://www.rosenlinks.com/IBIO/Khan

For Further Reading

Ananda, Mitra, Ph.D. *Digital Communications: From E-Mail to the Cyber Community* (The Digital World). New York, NY: Chelsea House, 2010.

Ananda, Mitra, Ph.D. *Digital Research: Inventing with Computers* (The Digital World). New York, NY: Chelsea House, 2011.

Anderson, Judith. *Education for All* (Working for Our Future). North Mankato, MN: Sea to Sea Publications, 2010.

Bartos, Judeen. *What Is the Role of Technology in Education?* (At Issue). Farmington Hills, MI: Greenhaven Press, 2012.

Brezina, Corona. *Sergey Brin, Larry Page, Eric Schmidt, and Google* (Internet Biographies). New York, NY: Rosen Publishing, 2012.

Byers, Ann. *Reid Hoffman and Linkedin* (Internet Biographies). New York, NY: Rosen Publishing, 2013.

Dobinick, Susan. *Mark Zuckerberg and Facebook* (Internet Biographies). New York, NY: Rosen Publishing, 2012.

Fisanick, Christina. *Education* (Teen Rights and Freedoms). Farmington Hills, MI: Greenhaven Press, 2011.

Furgang, Kathy. *Netiquette: A Student's Guide to Digital Etiquette* (Digital and Information Literacy). New York, NY: Rosen Central, 2010.

Gerber, Larry. *Cited!: Identifying Credible Information Online* (Digital and Information Literacy). New York, NY: Rosen Central, 2010.

Greek, Joe. *Writing Term Papers with Cool New Digital Tools* (Way Beyond Powerpoint: Making 21st-Century Presentations). New York, NY: Rosen Publishing, 2014.

Grinapol, Corinne. *Reed Hastings and Netflix* (Internet Biographies). New York, NY: Rosen Publishing, 2013.

Henningfeld, Diane Andrews. *Education* (Global Viewpoints). Farmington Hills, MI: Greenhaven Press, 2012.

Hubbard, Rita. *Getting the Most Out of MOOC: Massive Open Online Courses* (Digital and Information Literacy). New York, NY: Rosen Publishing, 2015.

Khan, Salman. *The One World Schoolhouse: Education Reimagined*. New York, NY: Grand Central Publishing, 2012.

Landau, Jennifer. *Cybercitizenship: Online Rights and Responsibilities* (Helpline: Teen Issues and Answers). New York, NY: Rosen Publishing, 2013.

Landau, Jennifer. *Jeff Bezos and Amazon* (Internet Biographies). New York, NY: Rosen Publishing, 2012.

Marcovitz, Hal. *Online Information and Research* (Issues in the Digital Age). San Diego, CA: Referencepoint Press, 2011.

Marzilli, Alan, and Victoria Sherrow. *Education Reform* (Point/Counterpoint). New York, NY: Chelsea House, 2011.

Meyer, Susan. *Jimmy Wales and Wikipedia* (Internet Biographies). New York, NY: Rosen Publishing, 2012.

Pascaretti, Vicki, and Sara Wilkie. *Team Up Online* (Super Smart Information Strategies). North Mankato, MN: Cherry Lake Publishing, 2010.

Popek, Emily. *Understanding the World of User-Generated Content* (Digital & Information Literacy). New York, NY: Rosen Central, 2010.

Rajczak, Kristen. *Instagram and Kevin Systrom and Mike Krieger* (Internet Biographies). New York, NY: Rosen Publishing, 2015.

Randolph, Ryan. *New Research Techniques: Getting the Most Out of Search Engine Tools* (Digital and Information Literacy). New York, NY: Rosen Central, 2011.

Rosa, Greg. *Databases: Organizing Information* (Digital and Information Literacy). New York, NY: Rosen Central, 2010.

Selingo, Jeffrey J. *College Unbound: The Future of Higher Education and What It Means for Students.* New York, NY: New Harvest, 2013.

Shea, Therese. *Steve Jobs and Apple* (Internet Biographies). New York, NY: Rosen Publishing, 2012.

Whiting, Jim. *Online Communication and Social Networking* (Issues in the Digital Age). San Diego, CA: Referencepoint Press, 2011.

Wilkinson, Colin. *Mobile Platforms: Getting Information on the Go* (Digital & Information Literacy). New York, NY: Rosen Central, 2011.

Young, Mitchell. *For-Profit Education* (Opposing Viewpoints). Farmington Hills, MI: Greenhaven Press, 2011.

Bibliography

Adams, Richard. "Sal Khan: The Man Who Tutored His Cousin—and Started a Revolution." *Guardian*, April 23, 2013. Retrieved March 4, 2014 (http://www.theguardian.com).

Bertodano, Helena de. "Khan Academy: The Man Who Wants to Teach the World." *Telegraph*, September 28, 2012. Retrieved March 4, 2014 (http://www.telegraph.co.uk).

Dreifus, Claudia. "It All Started with a 12-Year-Old Cousin." *New York Times*, January 27, 2014. Retrieved March 4, 2014 (http://www.nytimes.com).

Economist. "Flipping the Classroom." September 17, 2011. Retrieved March 4, 2014 (http://www.economist.com/node/21529062).

Friedell, Dan. "LeBron Teaches Kids via the Khan Academy." *ESPN Playbook*, December 1, 2012. Retrieved March 4, 2014 (http://espn.go.com).

High, Peter. "Education Technology Is in Its Infancy but It Is Growing Up Fast." *Forbes*, December 9, 2013. Retrieved March 4, 2014 (http://www.forbes.com).

High, Peter. "Salman Khan, the Most Influential Person in Education Technology." *Forbes*, January

6, 2014. Retrieved March 4, 2014 (http://www
.forbes.com).

Hof, Robert. "Comcast, Khan Academy Aim
Multimillion-Dollar Partnership at Low-Income
Families." *Forbes*, December 16, 2013. Retrieved
March 4, 2014 (http://www.forbes.com).

Kaplan, David A. "Bill Gates' Favorite Teacher."
Fortune, August 24, 2010. Retrieved March 4, 2014
(http://money.cnn.com).

Khan, Salman. "Let's Use the Video to Reinvent
Education." TED, March 2011. Retrieved March 4,
2014 (http://www.ted.com/talks/salman_khan
_let_s_use_video_to_reinvent_education).

Khan, Salman. "When Salman Khan Met Bill Gates."
Fortune, October 9, 2012. Retrieved March 4, 2014
(http://money.cnn.com).

Khan Academy Schools. "Khan Academy at the Los
Altos School District in Los Altos, CA." June 25,
2012. Retrieved March 4, 2014 (https://www
.youtube.com/watch?v=eJQzBJ6DtoY).

Oremus, Will. "A Q&A with Khan Academy Founder
Salman Khan." *Slate*, August 1, 2011. Retrieved
March 4, 2014 (http://www.slate.com).

Oremus, Will. "Salman Khan, Founder of Khan
Academy." *Slate*, August 2, 2011. Retrieved March
4, 2014 (http://www.slate.com).

Reich, Justin. "Don't Use Khan Academy Without Watching This First." *Education Week*, June 21, 2012. Retrieved March 4, 2014 (http://blogs .edweek.org).

Sengupta, Somini. "The Khan Academy Goes to Camp, and It's All Offline." *New York Times*, July 26, 2012. Retrieved March 4, 2014 (http://www.nytimes.com).

Sengupta, Somini. "Online Learning, Personalized." *New York Times*, December 4, 2011. Retrieved March 4, 2014 (http://bits.blogs.nytimes.com).

Strauss, Valerie. "How Well Does Khan Academy Teach?" *Washington Post*, July 27, 2012. Retrieved March 4, 2014 (http://www.washingtonpost.com).

Tan, Sarah. "Khan Academy Founder Returns Home as Big Name in U.S. School Reform." *Times-Picayune*, May 18, 2013. Retrieved March 4, 2014 (http://www .nola.com).

Temple, James. "Salman Khan, Math Master of the Internet." *SFGate*, December 14, 2009. Retrieved March 4, 2014 (http://www.sfgate.com).

Urstadt, Bryant. "Salman Khan: The Messiah of Math." *Bloomberg Businessweek*, May 19, 2011. Retrieved March 4, 2014 (http://www.businessweek.com).

Index

ABOUT THE AUTHOR

Ariana Wolff is a writer and world traveler with a background in indigenous studies and social pedagogy. Her areas of interest include education reform, social policy in developing countries, and non-Western literary movements. Wolff currently lives in Brooklyn, New York.

PHOTO CREDITS

Cover, p. 3 Bloomberg/Getty Images; pp. 6–7, 81 Jim Wilson/The New York Times/Redux; pp. 12, 37, 39, 44, 46, 69, 92, 93 Hope Lourie Killcoyne; pp. 16–17 Michael DeMocker/The Times-Picayune/Landov; p. 19 Alberto E. Rodriguez/Getty Images; p. 24 © iStockphoto.com/KingWu; p. 27 Piotr Adamowicz/Shutterstock.com; p. 29 Agencia Estado/AP Images; pp. 34–35 Steve Jennings/Getty Images; p. 52 Larry Busacca/WireImage/Getty Images; pp. 56–57 Ann E. Yow-Dyson/Archive Photos/Getty Image; pp. 59, 64 Leigh Vogel/WireImage/Getty Images; p. 67 Neilson Barnard/Getty Images; p. 71 © iStockphoto.com/Vidok; p. 77 Michael Nichols/National Geographic Image Collection/Getty Images; p. 86 Stephen Lam/Reuters/Landov; p. 97 © AP Images; cover and interior pages background image dpaint/Shutterstock.com; pp. 18–19, 25–26, 43–45, 60–61, 70–71, 76–77, 96–98 inset background image kentoh/Shutterstock.com.

Designer: Brian Garvey; Executive Editor: Hope Lourie Killcoyne; Photo Researcher: Karen Huang